Poems

T0303572

Hulk Church
Justin Lacour

Fort Smith, Arkansas

HULK CHURCH

Cover image: *Ghost of a Genius* by Paul Klee (1922).
Original public domain image from Wikipedia.
Digitally enhanced by rawpixel and modified by Belle Point Press.
Photograph: Detail of St. Joseph, Andrew Thornebrooke via Unsplash.

Author photograph: Kate Lacour

Edited by Casie Dodd
Design & typography by Belle Point Press

Belle Point Press, LLC
Fort Smith, Arkansas
bellepointpress.com
editor@bellepointpress.com

Find Belle Point Press
on Facebook,
Twitter (@BellePointPress),
and Instagram (@bellepointpress)

Printed in the United States of America

27 26 25 24 23   1 2 3 4 5

ISBN: 978-1-960215-07-9

CHAP8/BPP20

CONTENTS

something shines out from every darkness

—Charles Wright

Nobody's stronger than forgiveness.

—Franz Wright

Jesus
Our Jesus
Our Jesus a pincushion

—Novica Tadić,

translated by Charles Simic

ON READING TOMIE DEPAOLA'S
THE NIGHT OF LAS POSADAS

My toddler keeps pointing to the snow in the storybook.
Why is it so blue?
He loves the guitars and horns of *Las Posadas*,
the angels and devils—particularly the devils.
He loves the miracle: The real Mary and Joseph
with Christ in utero appear in the procession,
knock on door after door only to be told
"No room. No room,"
till finally the townspeople open a door
and they all parade into the light.
The people have their Christmas
and the Holy Family disappears
back into statues in the church,
only now their cloaks are dusted with snow
as proof of the miracle.

✝

There's cold, but no snow here.
My children go to sleep and I curl up
in bed. The lights go black.
If You are knocking, I can't hear it,
and I have no room for You right now.
I'm busy in a nest of empty beer cans,
fantasizing about a stranger
using me as a dog.
No matter how far I go,
all my dreams come back to chains.
My imagination will keep me out of heaven,
along with rage and hate,
but also the fear that keeps buzzing in my head.
The fear that never shuts up,
never leaves space for anything else.

✝

I want the quiet of snowfall for a moment,
the hopeful blankness of an earth covered in snow.
There is a real place—I've forgotten the way—
but there is a real place where You sleep
in a trough because there is no other place for You.
You sleep amid the smell of shit
and the stale heat of animals.
If I pick You up, head on my shoulder,
breath in my ear, You will not wake.
But will You dream of me? In gray strokes?
Or awash in color I've never known?
A new intensity. Another life.
Child who needs nothing,
but wants me to give everything.

MONDAY, 8:13 P.M.

At some point, things began to lose their meaning.

But not completely.

Greuze's *Broken Eggs*, where a maid mourns
her lost virginity, meant something.

Orpheus traveling through hell for love
meant something.

The church after a hurricane, lightless
and hot. Anorexic Christ on the cross.

And one day, the voice underneath all
the other voices will cry for me to
come back, cry like a needy child,
like a child being stabbed in the heart.

STATIONS

The time I spilled my whole bottle of Xanax
on the floor of a Jersey Transit train,
and had to white-knuckle it all the way
from Paterson back to Manhattan.

It was like a tree suddenly shedding every leaf:
Exposed, shivering thing.

I remember a tunnel that went on and on,
windows turning black.

I wanted to stick my panic in the hole
in Your side, like Thomas' finger,
let You swallow it away forever.

You suffered a darkness much darker than mine,

as if to say *I love you.*
Even if you never get better.
I love you.

HULK CHURCH

My four-year-old son asked, "Does the Hulk go to church?" I didn't know what to say. Maybe. Maybe, he goes to a special church with other Hulks. That way, the other parishioners aren't disturbed by the Hulks' loud, off-key singing, the fists pounding the pews in concurrence with the homily, the bare feet stamping in line for communion. It's a church that lets you scream; a church that lets you hold God in your enormous hands. I picture the Hulk cramming himself in the confessional, the walls bursting, as he bellows his sins through a metal screen. A voice on the other side gives absolution even though, like me, Hulk will do the same thing over again. I want to hear that voice. Not as a whisper, but as a scream louder than my screams.

SUNDAY, 6:56 A.M.

Might I suggest a nineties-era rom com
about me, an anorexic, and my slightly-more anorexic girlfriend.
I chugged SlimFasts and Marlboros
like someone's mom,
while she mixed Sweet'N Low in marinara sauce
and ate it with a spoon.
Lying down by the fire after my parents went to bed,
I reached out to cup her small breast,
brushed her ribs and thought
of a birdcage and a thousand
starving birds crying in her chest.
I loved her desperately,
but never made her life any better,
never stopped her hair from thinning out—
which is not love, just showing up.
I was a bystander like everybody else.
Later, she left me to join a cult.
The cult told her she could make no further progress
toward God with me in her life.
I don't know if that's right.
I believe in a great voice

telling me my life is not meaningless.
Sometimes, I have trouble hearing it.
When I was young, I heard it all the time.
I tried to win her back, playing "One" by U2
for her on my guitar, E-string snapping
before the critical third verse.
The verse about the "lepers in your head."
The verse that would have saved us.

TUESDAY, 7:39 P.M.

I'm thinking tonight of the professional
plasma donors, their workday finally ending.
Guys experienced enough
to bring blankets and snacks for the chair.
Guys hugged by the nurses hooking
them to blood-sucking machines.

I don't understand why the people I love
don't love me back, and yet, I get it.

I may start dipping my sandwich in water
before I chew it, like the competitive
eaters do; that could make a difference
or at least make things go a little smoother.

Some people post their workouts,
others bring their dogs to bars
(There may be some overlap here).

I do neither, but was a noted book thief

in my youth. Things were different back
then; you could get away with stuff.

Now, I sit in this garden I didn't plant.
My thoughts go from blood to gardens,
Eve and the poppies and sunlight of Eden.

I picture her hair long against her back,
like its dream was to slither down
to the earth, to lose itself in the new grass.
It thought there was enough time.

TUESDAY, 1:12 P.M.

I won't complain, but I will not lie either.
My stomach feels like a Coke machine shoved
down an elevator shaft by frat boys.

It's the Feast of St. Francis of Assisi.
My family is the only family unwelcomed
at the Blessing of the Pets.
We show up with snakes, lizards, etc.

When I have panic attacks though, I think of Francis
suffering, how once, in a vision, Christ unhooked
His hand from the cross and embraced Francis
to comfort him, though His own body was broken,
to teach Francis how much he was loved. Even then.

Look, I believe Christ will do this again.
He'll pull me close in the moment of my failure,
and I'll cry saltless tears. I'll learn to stop shaking.

SATURDAY, 11:22 A.M.

Gray, useless day, my children pitted one against the other,
and then, a memory:
New Year's Day 2004,
flying into Flint to visit my girlfriend and her parents,
touring Frankenmuth,
the town where it's Christmas all year long,
hungover and nauseous
with all the happy families.
The tinsel and lights are blurry now,
but I remember hating Michigan,
the snow, dry-humping in Fred and Pam's basement,
a single glass of cherry wine after dinner.
The memory is another child begging for my attention
on a cold day with too much rain, too little coffee.
There's nothing special or pleasant about this memory,
but it's one where I wasn't afraid or alone,
so it needs extra care to keep from dying.

MEDITATION (CUT THE MULLET!!!)

No one talks about Wesley Willis anymore. His songs used to waft through my dorm room. One time, he headbutted me clear across a tavern in Houston. I only stopped when I hit a wall and lost all capacity for metaphor. Showbiz is cruel. A giant gets on stage, sings songs like "Cut the Mullet" or "I Wupped Batman's Ass," and no one remembers. What bothers me isn't evanescence or the boredom of music in the following years; it's the suspicion we're busy telling the wrong stories, reliving the wrong memories. He performed bravely that night; half the crowd showed up to make fun of him.

Tonight's the night before New Year's Eve. Smoke from early fireworks. I won't go to sleep in my clothes this year. I want to be remembered, or, at least, not forgotten. I want to go find the people who used to love me and make them love me again. But it's too late for that. A glass of water and a baby aspirin. Branches hug the moon at this angle. Memory can be a type of forgiveness, a way of permitting someone to stay in your life another minute, rather than disappear. I don't want to disappear, until the day I love so much it won't matter who loves me back, then I can go.

MEDITATION
(NOT A THEOLOGY MAJOR, BUT . . .)

If someone were to nod off on the couch after seven beers, and wake to someone's tiny daughter covering him gingerly with her blanket, could he be forgiven for thinking of the Gerasene demoniac, how the man was naked and alone, but found fully clothed with Christ (perhaps because Christ gave the man His own cloak to wear), and how, after a moment of compassion, the man stopped howling and cutting himself in the land of the dead, and finally came back to his right mind?

SUNDAY, 10:25 A.M.

Five days sober, standing
in the church parking lot,
a stranger pulls up and
hands me a sticker: "I
am the BEST at who
I am!" and drives off.

I worry my hands will
tremble when I peel it
off and slap it on my shirt.

Please don't laugh.

I've fucked up so much.

The slightest forgiveness
nearly shatters me.

WEDNESDAY, 8:45 P.M.

If I had it to do over again,
I'd spend less time worrying
people were trying to poison me.
The time I threw away
perfectly good tofu, a breakfast shake.
The time on the phone with
poison control, the aspirin company.
I'd like that time back, and
it can be given to me.
There could be a time
when all my fears
dissolve like blood into an ocean.
I'd like to have that.
Please don't turn me away.

THURSDAY, 12:21 P.M.

When I was a teenager,
one of the brothers who taught
at my Catholic school
actually came to my house
because he was worried
how much I was drinking.
We took a walk on the levee
and watched the cargo ships
drifting up river, then
he told me it was okay
to be angry at God;
God can take it.

*

My God, I worry You've
made a world where one mistake
will cost me everything
and to trust You is to provoke
disaster, but here I am,
hiding in Your great shadow.
Today, for a moment, I flew
high above the old anger,
as if pulled by a team of small,
drab birds, their hearts bursting
to lift me off the ground.
I wanted to take everything back,
make my mind another sort
of storm, and give it to You.

ANOREXIC'S CANTICLE

Whatever I will drink
myself sick over,
there my treasure lies.

Whatever I will starve
myself for, there my
heart is.

I think it started with
a nest of fears, and then my
reaction, stupid and violent,
a bone-infecting violence,
a red sky violence.

But who remembers?

The reasons are less important
than the words that form
to beg my way out.

So, let's have a good cry.

Here's my humiliation standing
at the door like a nine-foot angel.

The beginning of wisdom.

But even if I never feel
Your healing breath,
let me still find some way to be
Your friend,

let me walk awake and alive
around Your unassailable beauty,

like these flowers floating on the pond
just before dark, with
a whisper of insects and
the trees swaying to cheer us on.

DIARY

I knelt down to draw pictures
with a lonely child today
for about twenty minutes,
animals wide-eyed with
stars for pupils.
It felt like forgiveness
for every day I was selfish
and afraid. A moment,
the color and light, I was
inexplicably in Your presence.
Later, a birdsong without anxiety,
a sunflower taller than me.

THE DEER

When I taught, I never had a car, so I'd ride the school van with
students. The van would pick us up at the train station, drive across
town, up a hill, through a thicket, and over to campus. The students
usually insisted on listening to something spirit-crushing on the
radio, like *Paternity Test Tuesday*, though occasionally the driver
would overrule them and play fifties countrypolitan. I sat alone
in the very back and tried not to make eye contact. It was a time
when just going to work made me feel I was about to collapse, and
I needed various pharmaceuticals to get over the anxiety of actually
teaching. One time though, as we were going through the woods, I
saw a deer on the side of the road, alert and staring at the van. Just
for a second, there was only the warm twang of steel guitars and
the deer's black eyes shining back at me, before she darted deeper
into the forest. I shouldn't make too much of things and, in that
part of Jersey, deer are basically considered vermin, but sometimes
I forget beauty and then it's there, like it never left. It's possible to
get so far away from beauty, it feels like someone else's life when
beauty comes up close again. And so this is a gift, this other life
of sunlight and trees and animals running from us through fallen
leaves. I've felt this before and since, but never asked to begin again

as something beautiful. Open my eyes now and let me wonder over the work of Your hands, but also over how everything responds to Your touch. Christ healed the leper. A deer cheered me up when I was sad. If You want to, You can make me clean.

WEDNESDAY, 7:17 A.M.

The goths are jogging again.
I've seen them before, but now
they seem sweet as the first star.
Two weeks sober,
I got up this morning
thinking of camp and how kids
would wake me up
by squatting over my head
and spreading their ass cheeks.
How they called it "red-eye."
How I just took it.
I didn't cry or split their faces
open with my fists
like those teenagers ten years ago
split my face open
off Magazine Street, not for money
or revenge, but because they could.
So now I look over my shoulder,
at what might be coming,
hoping for the ordinary
boredom: The green flash

when I close my eyes too fast,
a garden gnome holding
what appears to be a trout,
the goths of summer
running toward a rising sun.

LITTLE FLOWER

A truck stop featuring karaoke. An uncle stockpiling gold.
     A trailer park called "Wheel Estates."

Any one of these is worth your attention, like a pin lost in a sea
     of grass is worth your attention.

It's the night before the first day of school. A treehouse
     chiaroscuro in the distance.

A boy & girl sit on the pedestrian bridge,
     splitting a thimble of marijuana,

their legs dangling over oblivion.
     The cars streaks of pure light below.

In the last hours of summer, a man with no arms
     takes a seat at a diner,

lights a cigarette with his feet.
     No one is born to be a symbol,

just born to be wildflowers
    fed and broken by the sun.

Here's a photo of you
    with your hair down. You are disguised

as Joan of Arc, your armor
    made of cloth, your wooden sword.

There's a battle you fight by becoming small.
    I need to start fighting.

There's something brave
    about being small.

And I want to be brave.

MEDITATION (ROAD TRIP)

I dated a woman who, like me, loved to drive and drive for the sake of driving, so whenever we had a free day, we'd just take off and go. One time, we ended up in a small town in Appalachia. The only thing to do there was visit the cemetery. We spent an hour walking among headstones: Graves with Disney characters chiseled in them; graves with little league trophies next to them. I didn't have the decency to cry, but at least kept my mouth shut, while we stumbled through that afternoon, strips of heat pulsing through the trees, the roar of coal trucks downshifting on the highway, our long drive back north. We tried for another month to drink through the distance between us, but couldn't last.

Twenty years later, in the middle of a plague, I drove across the lake to buy rabbit skins for my wife to stuff. Besides a trunkful of frozen rabbits, the farmer handed me a Chick tract about hell to read, which I did, sitting in the car, taking in the black-and-white flames. I love many things I shouldn't love. Now, it's time to drive back across the deep water separating me from my home, my kids washing for dinner, my wife finally sitting down. The sun is beginning to set. I hope for a silence before the great silence. A time when I can hear the One Who formed my heart, when I can cry for a hurt other than my own. For the distant hearts and broken roads and graves decorated like children's rooms.

I'm sorry I never wanted the life I've been given, never recognized Your sun shining like a healing.

May I sense a little of the light breaking in from another world and awake, surprised by mercy.

PRAYER BEFORE DAWN

Lord,

excuse my night sweats;

let my eyes adjust first.

I want to go back to sleep,

but it is almost time to give up

and face the day.

✝

I have tried for years to be well,
that is, the person You want me to be.

I don't know how to come into the light.

I remember Caravaggio's *The Calling of St. Matthew*,
how Matthew keeps his head down, counting
money, sitting in the shadows,
till Christ points to him, fingers curled
as if Christ wants to pull Matthew out of his seat.
But Matthew listens; he gets up; he follows.

I've seen that painting a thousand times,
light invading the dark of the customs post.
Christ visiting uninvited.

I don't know how I can see beautiful things
and still wallow in ugliness.

Sometimes, I'd rather disappear than change.

✢

I almost disappeared for real
the years I stopped eating.

I stopped eating because
I was afraid of being less than perfect,

which meant I was always afraid.

The time I tried to swim the lake:
halfway through, my body gave out,
arms and legs too thin to carry
me across. Stuck, flailing like
an insect on its back, gulping black
water, as gravity tugged me down.

But this wasn't the emergency
I secretly longed for. No toned
lifeguard fished me out.
I just bobbed back to shore,
spent the afternoon sitting on a towel,
pretending I was a regular adult.

✢

You can be content to be sick.

I am not content.

I am exhausted keeping up with being sick,
and wish for an incision in my brain,
a doctor to rip out the obsessions,
someone to fix me.

✢

There is a light and it is Your light.

I starved myself and never saw it,
but today it's here, entering under my roof,
washing over my humiliation.

Not just a feeling—there is a change,
what I could never do myself.

The unexpected, undeserved light.

And I will live because of this light,
and eat and grow strong again.

The day is coming.

Have mercy on me.

COMING HOME

St. Francis used to roll in the snow
to shake off lust.

I should try something like that.

I could make angels on the lawn
before my fantasies spiral into darkness.

The sweetness of this commute,
it cuts deep.

Like hearing Syd Barrett's "Gigolo Aunt" on the radio
is a deep cut,
"Achy Rakey Heart" by Eugene Chadbourne and Evan Johns
is a deep cut.

But not as deep as the hawk gliding over I-10,

not as deep as the man with a metal rod
for a leg, begging at the off-ramp,

who is not a prop for this poem,
but a candle in a sea of screens,

up there with fireflies landing
on my sweater when I was single, and

the woman at mass wearing
a bicycle helmet just in case
she falls down.

MALACHI 3:24

—He will turn the hearts of fathers to their sons

My children are playing a game
that's actually a creative way
to injure three people at once.

A bungee cord.
Six clothes hangers.
A mini-trampoline.

Excuse me, I need to stop them,

but before I do,
thank You for slowly turning
my heart back to my children,

away from the wages of depression.

Thank You for calling me back
from the edge of anger and panic.

One day, I'll tell them.

How miracles don't always
happen in an instant.

The little miracles
are like cracks in my windshield:

the initial impact growing
wider and deeper with time,

until I will dream of nothing,
but You and this life I've been given.

Acknowledgments

Some of these poems appeared in *Amethyst Review, Cherry Tree, Concision, Ekstasis, Fou Magazine, Presence, Red Ogre Review, Reformed Journal, South Dakota Review,* and *The Windhover.* Many thanks to the editors and staff of these journals.

No end of gratitude to my wife, Kate Lacour, who first read/critiqued these poems. She is a bright shining light, and this book is for her and our three children, Hank, Ozzie, and Harlan.

Also thankful to Brittany Lacour, Colleen Rothman, Danny Unger, LeeAnna Callon, Mary Ann Miller, Nikki Ummel, and Michelle Nicholson for their kindness and encouragement in a dark time.

An unpayable debt to my parents who first introduced me to books and kept poetry in the house for me to discover. Their love and faith are a continual blessing.

Most of the poems were written during my children's Christmas break (2022). I'm thankful for this time. There was plenty of noise, Bob Dylan, Van Morrison, Joe Henry, Hank Williams, and Sharp's non-alcoholic beer. Golden days in the healing game.

Thanks to Casie Dodd for reading these poems and giving them a home. Your generosity means the world.

Justin Lacour lives in New Orleans with his wife and three children. He is the editor of *Trampoline: A Journal of Poetry*.